BEN

SUCH A BLESSING TO
BE WITH YOU
X
Joanna.

MIND BODY SPACES

A GUIDE TO NEXT LEVEL ALIGNMENT

JOANNA JAMES

Copyright © 2020 Joanna James
First published in Australia in 2020
by Karen McDermott
Waikiki, WA 6169

All rights reserved. No part of this book may be used or reproduced by any means, graphic, electronic, or mechanical, including photocopying, recording, taping or by any information storage retrieval system without the written permission of the copyright owner except in the case of brief quotations embodied in critical articles and reviews.

Although the author and publisher have made every effort to ensure that the information in this book was correct at press time, the author and publisher do not assume and hereby disclaim any liability to any party for any loss, damage, or disruption caused by errors or omissions, whether such errors or omissions result from negligence, accident, or any other cause.

National Library of Australia Cataloguing-in-Publication data:
Mind Body Spaces/Joanna James
Success/Self-help

ISBN: (sc)
ISBN: (e)

Dedication:

This book is dedicated to humanity.

My intention is that it illuminates this world, soothes many souls and inspires them to become all that they can possibly be.

I am eternally grateful to all the magnificent beings who support me so beautifully in this journey called life.

To my magnificent mentors, Ron and Caroline, who believed in me during my darkest hour and encouraged me to share who I am with the world.

To Brendan, for the countless hours of supportive patience and loving edits.

To my family by blood, birth and beyond, who love me through thick and thin.

To Peter, for sharing and teaching me so many of life's loves and lessons.

To Nicole, for your dedication to educating the planet on healthy homes.

To Katina, for nothing is ever too bizarre to share.

To Lisa, for your continual acceptance and encouragement.

To Mikael, Ariel and all the Archangels for blessing me with your presence.

To you, for being receptive to the information contained within. May it serve and guide you on your journey into **Next Level Alignment**.

Joanna James

CONTENTS

Life is a Spiral	7
MIND	**11**
Space and Creativity	13
The Energetics of your Business	18
Creating Results Intentionally	24
So if it's so simple, then why is it not so simple?	29
Aligning your mind	32
Shirley's Case Study	*35*
Reflection/Creation Exercise	*37*
BODY	**41**
The Doorway between the Physical and Spiritual	43
Physical Space and your Health	50
Mould	52
Electromagnetic Fields	55
EMF and Cancers	58
Brain Tumours	59
Hypersensitivity	60
Building Materials	63
Space and Your Relationships	66
Clearing Your Energy	70
Roger's Case Study	*75*
Release and Invoke Exercise	*77*

SPACES 79
So exactly what is energy? 81
Mapping Your Energy Signature 84
Your Inner Guidance System 87
Achieving Your Bliss 94
Next Level Alignment 97
The 12 Universal Laws in Simple Explanation. *100*

References 101

> *"The human mind always makes progress,*
> *but it is a progress in spirals."*
> MADAME DE STAEL

LIFE IS A SPIRAL

I'm seriously convinced life is one giant spiral. In fact, the past few years have proven it to me beyond any doubts. I have revisited places, people and circumstances within the definitive patterns that show life to be an expansion of movement, always with a familiar twist of deja vu.

So exactly what is a spiral?

According to the great Universal Law of Correspondence, it expresses patterns on all planes of existence, from the smallest electron to the brightest star. This universal law is often used to explain the concept of as is above, so is below, or the notion our outer world reflects our inner world. More simply, it explains the repeating patterns in life. Spirals are evidenced everywhere in nature.

As a mathematical principle, a spiral creates an ever-expanding curve that, over time, gains greater and greater distance from its centre. I have found this can also be experienced as a perspective or wisdom as we revisit places, events or interact with people from an expanded perspective. Albeit from a similar locale or familiar setting, and so the patterning of life events often emulate the form of a spiral.

As equiangular spirals increase their shape, they remain the same with each rotation of their curve, such as the great spiral of the galaxy. Perhaps it's this patterning of events that creates the greatest sense of deja vu as life unfolds with a sense of being of similar ratio, but different. I have concluded life is one giant spiral expressed as we, too, spiral through the spiralling galaxy.

This leads me to wonder what the experiences of life might be if we were to travel upon a renowned Fibonacci Spiral or even a Golden Spiral. How would the events of our life be different if it were possible to choose which type of spiral we are to traverse upon?

When we move through a rapid period of accelerated growth, is this a Fibonacci spiral? *A Fibonacci sequence is based on a numerical sequence adding the preceding two numbers to get the next 0, 1, 1, 2, 3, 5, 8, 13, 21, 34, etc.* Should we feel a divine pathway unfolding, could this a period of Golden proportions?

To the untrained eye, one might be coerced into believing the increasing proportions of the Fibonacci and the golden spiral are the same. Yet they are based on two different formulas. The Fibonacci is an increasing numerical sequence as described above and depicted below.

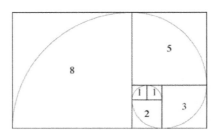

A golden spiral is based on the formula for the Golden Mean 1.618 and shows increasing rectangles represented by the formula below.

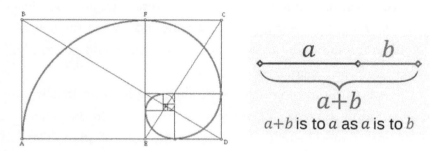

Albeit similar in creation, who is to say what life is like traversing on one and not the other?

Much like riding a bike, what facilitates the changes of gears in life enabling us to traverse between different movements and life experiences?

Not surprisingly, this is where the Universal Law of Rhythm seems to come into play, demonstrating all things move in cycles.

As I reflect on the markers that are the cycles of my life, I cannot help but notice where I am physically, mentally, emotionally and spiritually located. The duration of time may vary from daily to monthly to yearly to a decade to several decades like a giant mandala with different parts of the picture completing at varying rates. No wonder we as humans are often so confused.

When I find myself in these points of introspection along the moving spiral of life, I have often taken a moment to integrate the meaning I am choosing to make of it all. That is the meaning in that precise moment of life journey.

Many years ago, I was blessed with the experience of studying with a bio- energetic meditation master who introduced to me the joys of the ancient art of spinning. And so, I set about simulating the ancient Sufi masters. Secretly wishing to look as graceful as I'd seen in the videos of gently dancing scarves, I would, however, fall often and also purge. I'd vomit violently as I was gripped with the nauseous fear of losing my centre. After several days and as many bruises, ironically, everything shifted profoundly when the master explained to me to let go and trust the energy would go exactly where it needed to go.

It was within this moment of freedom I realised we are always connected to the centre of our own universe. And in the greatest moment of movement there is always the core of stillness and connection. This continues to be one of the greatest gifts I have been fortunate to receive in this lifetime and has become a regular practice to maintain my sense of energetic centre. In everyday life when challenges present, I remind myself I am at a different point on the giant spiral, and that this too, shall pass. Life's movement allows things to unfold into a new perspective, knowing I am always connected to the Universal Centre.

When we realise the fundamental relationships we have to space, we are then afforded the opportunity to explore our relationship to the spaces we inhabit. We learn how they hold the hidden keys to unlocking golden pathways within the great Spiral of life. Who would have thought the clues so many desperately seek are right before our very eyes?

MIND

"But out of limitations comes creativity."
DEBBIE ALLEN

SPACE AND CREATIVITY

If you take the time to examine the definition of space, you will find an inherent juxtaposition. On one hand, you will find it described as an expanse that is unoccupied or available. On the other hand, we also describe it as the three-dimensional realm within which all things exist. It is this dynamic relationship of existence/non-existence that allows space to be the perfect stage to enact all the universal laws.

We think of creativity as the artistic side of life and that we either have it or we don't. Further influenced by the indoctrination of many of the world's education systems, we are often told we are proficient at logic or intuition, but rarely both. Rarely are we taught that creativity is a universal ability applicable to any modality and that every human being is naturally gifted with one's own unique creative abilities.

In my early days of architectural practice, I would observe many couples who created a new home together. The dynamics of each unique relationship always brought a mixture of personalities and skill sets. It always amazed me how at least one person in the partnership gave up their claim to their innate creativity. Ironically, with the right conditions, it was usually this client who would often regather the splintered parts of their creative self throughout the process of creating a new space.

The creative process is one that gives form to the yet unrealised. Human beings create their reality first mentally, so in this sense, imagination is key. As Catherine Ponder explained in the early 1970s, manifesting is 98 percent mental and only 2 percent action. With this staggering percentage in mind, we can see the role mindset has to play in the results of one's life. In truth, we are all creating our lives every single second of every single day which underpins such statements like "power is in the present moment." It is essential we understand the physical spaces we attract and create are a direct reflection of our way of being. Spaces are a direct barometer of how we create in life.

There are always clues within our physical space that indicate how we are creating on a subconscious level. Understanding the correlation between what we are aware of and what we hide can often be tricky, especially when there are many layers to consider before energy rests into physical form. Beyond the visible dimensions, lie the energetic patterns of both ideas/thoughts and feelings/emotions. Even after energy rests into physical form, the surrounding energetics to which we expose it to can still influence it.

A simple example of this might be a home space you walk into and you immediately feel happy or you feel at peace and relaxed. In contrast, we have all experienced a space we felt uncomfortable in, contracted or confronted in, as though there was something about the space that was encroaching upon us, making one feel uneasy.

Each built space uniquely combines energetic patterns and

events that create its signature. This is tangible to those trained to know how to decipher it.

A study by the Karolinska Institute in Sweden has evidenced our mind can use imagination to alter our perception of reality. Christopher Beger explains, "We often think about the things we imagine and the things we perceive as being clearly dissociable. However, what this study shows is that our imagination of a sound or a shape changes how we perceive the world around us in the same way hearing that sound or seeing that shape does. Specifically, we found that what we imagine hearing can change what we see, and what we imagine seeing can change what we hear."

If we model the physical spaces we create and dwell in on our thoughts and feelings, then they, too, are programmable as an extension of our imagination. This idea extends well beyond the contemporary idea of covering a wall with a thousand post-it notes of positivity. It moves into the realm of supercharging our environments according to the meaning our imagination makes of them.

The programming or decoding of spaces is a fascinating process to undertake and one used by masters since the beginning of time. In the fundamentals of Feng Shui, it is understood that all things have a flow of Qi (Chi) being energy. I have witnessed many times how energetic patterns have had a direct effect on the occupants of the space. Once mapped and identified, we can reprogram these spaces to offer a different arrangement of potentiality.

Equally, spaces have a direct effect on the potential to be creative. On a simple level, light, colour, mood and ambience can substantially change the way one can feel able to be creative.

For many years as we expanded our business, I would test these theories on the layout of our team within the office. As the business was growing rapidly, we often needed to relocate staff as departments grew and new people joined us. In one particular western office, we'd a particularly challenging energetic pattern. I watched with fascination as the energetic imprint for conflict and arguments systematically affected *every person in a detrimental way* who was located in that office. Almost at the point that I was to turn it into a filing room with no occupants. We hired an in-house legal counsel who flourished within this energy as it supported and nourished his argumentative flare in a constructive manner.

Another key to the mastery of Feng Shui is the realisation there are three levels of luck: human, earthly and heavenly. Just like differing DNA and potential immunity, each person will have a unique response to the effects of a physical space. In my experience, the universal influences are an overriding energetic system that will display repeated themes of influence or experience regardless of individual disposition.

The Universal Law of Attraction states it's a like-attracts-like vibration. While this has been often explained relative to opportunities, people and mantras for attracting money into one's life, many don't realise we attract spaces in exactly the same way. Every space we inhabit comes into our life like a magnet to replicate the energetic vibration we are emitting. The space acts a mirrored container to demonstrate the energetic patterns we focus upon whether we are aware of them. Concurrently, the manner with which we create life whilst we occupy a particular space is equally under direct influence of the physical space. Hence spaces directly affect the manner in which we manifest and create.

Any person choosing to create a difference in their life must without exception look at the spaces they inhabit and create a difference in the physical forms within the space first.

Remember, physical space is moving, vibrating energy that can be engaged with and influenced under the right conditions. Not too dissimilar to a Monet painting, often the overall picture can only be seen from a unique vantage point. However, without each individual dot of colour, the overall image will form differently. In this way, we can then see the relevance of every object, wall and room form in the overall experience of one's life.

> *"The space in which we live should be for the person we are becoming now, not the person we were in the past."*
> MARIE KONDO

THE ENERGETICS OF YOUR BUSINESS

If every physical space we encounter has its own unique energetic imprint, then it's a logical conclusion to see our personal energetic field will be affected by the spaces in which we find ourselves. And the manner in which we experience prosperity. It is also logical to see the physical spaces holding our businesses will also have a profound effect on the people who work there and on the nature and success of the business itself.

I have watched curiously over many years, observing the cycles of how our business has shifted and changed relative to the office space we have placed it within. The container of a business from my experience will be experienced in the following three areas:

1. The Physical Container – the space itself
2. The Mental Container – the figurehead and belief systems of the business

3. The Emotional Container - the people and their feelings about the business

I remember many years ago searching for a new office space to lease in Sydney. With my list of budget constraints and size requirements, I set about to negotiate and create the perfect container for our new offices. Overarching this was the need to find a building with the best energetic chart I could find, optimising the business wealth potential as much as possible. Having explained the very specific needs for exact completion dates, orientation and entry points to many real estate agents, I became immune over time to the doubtful and sometimes condescending reactions to my requests. Determined to prove the success of the venture, we eventually signed a lease in a newly completed space in the southern end of the city. This was a bold move to step away from the Central CBD. However, it offered many other advantages including ease of access and amenities for the team, alongside the perfect stage for my energetic experiment.

As we started the fit out and staffing for the new office, I explained to all the team members how lucky we were to have found a space with such a strong potential for success. I also explained the choice of colours and furniture and how each aspect would support and contribute to the potential growth of the business.

Whilst the physical space is an essential component, the figurehead or space-holder is of equal importance too, and so we relocated one of our key managers to Sydney to lead and develop the new division. His drive and ambition were unquestionable, and quickly the business volumes grew beyond our expectations.

Finally, as everyone in the team could see the team growing and expanding, this added to the satisfaction and expression of success each member experienced whilst working within the space. The final element of emotion engagement from the team added a layer of undeniable vitality to the business space and the results of the business itself.

Which aspect—the physical, mental or emotional came first—or which aspect had the greatest influence is hard to say. One thing beyond question is that the intricate interconnectedness of all three elements in my estimation were crucial to the success of the business at the time.

One of my favourite sayings is, "The fish stinks from the head down." The energetics of the business leader whether they be the owner, CEO or potentially another leader, or series of leaders in a team are the people who set the energetic experience for the business. These are the people ultimately responsible for the energetic health or success of the organisation. The primary responsibility of all business leaders is to do whatever it takes to be clear about their own dynamic relationship to the business. Whenever there is something amiss in a business, the first place to look is within those who are leading the business direction.

Similar to a physical space, a business reflects energetics as the total contributions of the people who work within the business. This is what I call collaborative energetics as the direct experience of every person within that organisation adds to the flavour, outcome and reality of the organisation. To achieve exceptional results in a business, this requires exceptional clarity and alignment. This process can sometimes be confronting particularly for those who look for reasons outside of themselves, rather than taking responsibility for what one contributes to the creative process.

When there is difficulty within a business in the form of disharmony, then there will be an area in one's life directly reflecting the same energetic vibration. This is governed by the Law of Correspondence, which states every action has a corresponding reaction. Just like the ripple effect of a stone entering a pond, a simple change in a physical space will create a corresponding energetic reaction.

Often, we are told work is completely independent of personal experience when the opposite could not be truer. All engagement within any business is still an energetic exchange originating from one's personal experience of life. And one's personal development of energetic expression will have a direct impact on the expression and experience of that person within the context of the business.

Whether we create in a physical form or whether we create through mastery in business, the same universal principles govern it. It takes courage, discipline and determination to continue to review oneself impartially. These qualities are usually demonstrable in any person of notable success.

Becoming aware of how space affects our performance results, both positively and potentially detrimental, is another tool available to any business. Once we understand the principles, business owners can reverse engineer the dynamics of their workspaces to create change that will inspire, motivate, energise the business towards realising its future success.

This is something that requires ongoing attention as all pieces of the energetic puzzle are in constant motion. This includes the state of one's desks, to the storeroom clutter, to the mindset of the CEO and the multiplicity of business dynamics to be managed in any given timeframe.

Just as it is so important to forecast budgets and business volumes, it is equally important to provide a container that can attract the desired business growth. Whether it be a desk in a sole trader's home or a multi-floor fit-out, understanding how the energetics of a business will translate into physical form is essential.

As a burgeoning design student in my 20s, the sleek lines of modernism and the latest trendy design theories and colour palettes bedazzled me. As we eagerly compared notes on the latest fad, I soon discovered the enormous responsibility that comes with creating spaces and the everyday user experience. A criticism of architects and the profession generally is the wide divide between the imagination of the drawing board (or computer these days) and the reality of the built form. Imagine if designers were expected to be given a brief to create a space that ensures maximum potential for economic success of a business too. That would be a game changer.

With the recent introduction of the Well Building Standards by Delos in 2014, the world understands how important it is to provide work spaces that are supportive to the overall health and wellbeing of the people who occupy them. With seven categories, the elements they look at range from water, air and light through to nourishment, mind and comfort. A quick perusal of their home page will lead you to questions such as, "Can the light in an office space help reduce stress and explain how meditation and sound can improve stress and focus?" Whilst the Well standard is an innovative tool for examining a new paradigm of building and an amazing shift in the consciousness, there are many factors that need to be included. For example, they should be used in conjunction when considering office spaces and the overall health and wellbeing of its occupants.

In the digital age, we are rapidly reliant on wireless technology and are obsessed with the amount of data and speed at which we can transmit information. We are yet to realise the extent of factors that will take effect upon our businesses. With the recent deployment and roll out of 5g across the Australian network, much marketing has been positioned to promote greater work efficiencies. However, few discussions occur on the potential liabilities of a workforce affected the measurable effects of the new levels of EMF. Given there are several scientific papers evidencing potential health effects including symptoms such as brain fog, fatigue and lack of memory, it is hard to imagine the impending environment of expanded WIFI will enhance the quality of future workspace environments regardless of download speeds.

JOANNA JAMES

"Remember how imperative it is to master emitting your own frequency and intention rather than absorbing energetic imprints from everyone else."
MARAYAAM HASNAA

CREATING RESULTS INTENTIONALLY

With all things in life, it is a question of clarity that drives results. If you cannot see how spaces are affecting you, then you cannot see the solutions that also surround you. As our energetic field becomes enmeshed within the spaces we inhabit, it becomes normal that our field of vision has also become enmeshed too. In this way, often a stranger can step into a space and observe the most obvious of things about the space that the occupant has become completely unaware of over time. The analogy of the frog in a pot who slowly but surely moves closer and closer to his impending death with each degree that the water warms is not too dissimilar.

Refining or redefining or gaining a new perspective on how we experience things clearly is essential as we engage our creativity and our passion to create new things in life. Whether it be new concepts, new relationships or new endeavours, they all stem from our ability to have clarity around the way we create.

Spaces are inherently reflective and hold the keys like a treasure chest that can show us the way forward. In a tale as old as time, the outlandish adventurer travels the seas to find the hidden treasure chest But what if it were sitting underneath the board table the entire time?

The ability to step outside of one's space and view the picture from a new perspective is similar to stepping outside of oneself to observe oneself in an entirely different paradigm. Perhaps for those who struggle to be the observer of our thoughts as often taught in mindfulness or meditation, a different course of action might be to become the observer of our space.

Once the energetic patterns and elements are seen clearly, this opens the gateway for the opportunity to rearrange the physical forms to allow future events to unfold in a different order. This is much like the scene in the Matrix when Neo realises he can morph the field as the fabric of the events change upon his command. As the physical objects within a space are moving at a slower rate of motion or vibration, it affords us more time to observe the shifts in form. Imagine yourself as Neo in slow motion as you move objects in space. You are also shifting anything associated with that object in terms of meaning or beliefs, too. When we remove an object which is seen to be symbolic of a situation or event you wish to remove from your life, three things occur:

1. You become conscious of a decision you are making about a specific area of your life, and because of the requirement for action, you set that desire into motion.
2. You create a vacuum which results in the inflow of new matter into that space.

3. As we witness the events unfold, the subconscious mind expects something new and sees this as validation a positive change is underway. Therefore it expects more changes to occur aligning one's frame of reference to the desired outcome.

The cycle of change can then create a self-fulfilling prophecy. As the space is changed, and changes are realised, then the belief in those changes becomes stronger, promoting a continued confidence in more changes.

Tony Robbins is a master of manifesting results in life. If you have ever attended one of his workshops, you will hear his booming voice instruct you to "change your state." This means a change in physiology that can help to then shift your focus of energy and associated emotions. We can think of objects in space as an extension of our physiology, so if you want to shake things up, "change your space." Humorously, this also usually requires a change of physiology to do so too.

So how do we best create intentional results?

Unfortunately for most of us on the planet, while we set about with the best of intentions to create results, it's the stew of our sub-consciousness thoughts that work against us. Our fabulous intentions quickly lead to frustration as it leaves us with a blinding headache from hitting our head against the brick wall of our hidden subconscious beliefs. Belief systems are nothing more than recurring patterns of thoughts. In this sense, they are a recurrence of energy we generate and transmit into the world, directly creating the results of our life. To be intentional with our results, we must be intentional with our beliefs, which drives our mindset, behaviour and outcomes.

Those things (thoughts) which hold us back are the things we must let go of to create the business success (results) we seek. This can only occur when we clear a space for new energy to flow into, otherwise there cannot be space for expansion.

Fundamentally, for your business to grow, you must grow too. We so often talk about accountability and responsibility within the corporate arena. However, rarely do we call or teach how to be accountable and responsible to ourselves.

For a business to thrive, it must undergo the same ongoing maintenance any physical space requires to be energetically clear. Attention must be placed on the energetic health of a business including the energetics of all the people operating within the business, too. While we express energetic health in the physical, mental and emotional realms, its origin starts within the metaphysical realm. The term "so be it" states whatever we accept or believe will take form. The translation of belief into results is merely the realisation of energetic thought patterning witnessed through a process of realisation.

It is throughout the interplay of the Universal law of Attraction (like attracts like) that we experience the results of our true business beliefs.

Within this process, it is not uncommon to be challenged as the universe sends back to the business the same challenges that lie unresolved within the energetic patterning of those shaping the business. Not exactly a normal boardroom conversation, however, it's exactly what is often needed in a boardroom conversation as leaders respond to business positioning and day-to-day challenges. Regardless, they are working through their own personal patterning, too.

When we hire CEO's, we look for dynamic leaders with relevant industry experience. However, rarely do we interview for an understanding of their own belief patterning.

"Manifesting is a lot like making cake. The things needed are supplied by you, the mixing is done by your mind and the baking is done in the oven of the universe."
STEPHEN RICHARDS

SO IF IT'S SO SIMPLE, THEN WHY IS IT NOT SO SIMPLE?

Creating results intentionally requires a key ingredient—a leap of faith. Beyond all the practical day-to-day planning or mastery of business execution, there must be a moment of pure belief. A steadfast commitment to knowing beyond any doubt the business will create the results it has declared (so be it). The ability of its leaders to communicate and emulate the embodiment of the future outcome will determine the proportion of critical mass of the people within the organisation to also "buy in" to the faith in the outcome.

We can describe courage as the commitment to action in the face of doubt. So regardless of the presentation of evidence to the contrary, a successful business leader must display courage to the business's convictions.

The Law of Inspired Action states we must take action to realise the Law of Attraction. It rolls quickly off the tongue.

However, the intricacies of the additional word 'inspired' is the essential thing to bring awareness too. Action that is forced or given begrudgingly will not bring inspired results. When people in a business are forced to take action that is out of alignment with their own personal beliefs, it creates tension unlikely to empower results. However, when people in a business see inspired action in motion, it adds a tangible momentum and creates an energetic field that others can feel and experience. This encourages others to participate in the compounding effect of the inspired action.

There is much debate around the shifting landscape of the Millennials' perception of business and leadership. According to a recent survey by **Deloitte Millennial Survey** released May 15, 2018, a survey of 10,455 millennials and 1,844 Gen Z youth revealed that:

- 75% believe leaders/business focus on their own agendas rather than considering the wider society.
- 62% think leaders/businesses have no ambition beyond wanting to make money.

Rather than a millennial character assassination, we could see this as a new form of expression by the rising masses for a different type of inspired leader. One with whom they can connect with and commit to follow.

So what does it take to be an inspired leader?

This is where intuition enters the logical realm of business. Learning to balance the logical mind with intuitive knowing is mastering the creation of exceptional results. It is intuition that drives a leap of faith, not logic. Another way of stating this might be that the rational mind will create rational results, the combined intuitive mind can create exponential results. Encouraging business leaders to follow their gut is becoming more and more the norm as the importance of EQ is recognised as well as IQ.

Deepak Chopra explains intuition is a form of intelligence that connects to a greater form of intelligence without fear. Intuition has a sense of clarity and guides us to make evolutionary choices. It is when this ability is combined with logic and reason that we can deliver exceptional results.

"Your Destiny is wherever you are, you see. The Universe has the ability to converge your magnificent life wherever you are. You do not need to be in a specific place or even with specific people. You just need to be specifically in alignment with Self."
ABRAHAM HICKS

ALIGNING YOUR MIND

If you review the definition of alignment in the Cambridge dictionary the first definition states:

"Arrangement in a straight line or in correct or appropriate relative positions."

However, the second definition is even more interesting:
"A position of agreement or alliance."

To postulate we can, in our minds, have everything in the correct position at any one time really is unimaginable. More so given the multiplicity of positions in which the mind could potentially be aligned due to the variety of thoughts we have had over the many years of our existence. It is estimated we experience between

60,000 and 80,000 thoughts per day. A quick calculation being almost forty-eight-years old means potentially I have had over 1400 million thoughts move through my mind in my lifetime. To attempt to align this volume of thoughts in one particular or correct order is overwhelming and so that is not the type of alignment of which I speak.

Compound this with the concept of the universal mind, we must consider the possibility that up to 90% of the thoughts entering our minds are not necessarily even ours. It is a staggering realisation when we embrace the task of being on twenty-four-hour patrol at the door of our very own minds, when the burglar is already well and truly inside the home.

For many years I found it crazy making, jumping at the shadows of my imagination with hyper vigilance only to then fall into the exhausted slumber of a comatose zombie. I can see now the effects on my life when my mind was not aligned to positive outcomes and the results when it clearly was.

The alignment I am speaking of is one where we understand whether the thoughts in our mind are actually in alignment with our most prized values and desires. And that the recurring patterns of thoughts form beliefs we wish to create in life.

Esther Hicks takes this concept even further and talks about alignment to the Source of all things, whether it be described as God, spirit, or the universe. She describes alignment as a position of alliance with one's true self.

And so here enters the sixth universal law, "the Perpetual transmutation of Energy." Bob Proctor explains this beautifully when he describes "energy is forever moving into form through form and back into form." A scientific explanation might be that of a blue sky, then the formation of clouds, the darkening of those clouds to deliver rain and then the water droplets over time evaporating back into the sky.

Another way of examining this is to understand the thoughts we are thinking are moving into physicality. As we create our own reality moment to moment, the thoughts we sanction manifest into physical forms within space. The physical forms of our space are a direct creation of our thoughts, whether we are conscious of them. This is why we can see the outline of our unclear thinking by the objects within our space that demonstrate a resonance which is unclear with our outcomes or desires.

When faced with the realisation that ultimately, we must take responsibility for every thought that passes, choosing to accept or to release and let it go, we are participating in creating all material forms within space. This requires a tremendous amount of commitment to concentration of a unique kind.

Geshe Kelsang Gyatso shares that the main function of virtuous concentration "Makes the Mind Peaceful." He explains that pure concentration helps to create a suppleness or flexibility and ease when using the mind. Perhaps it is in this use of mind that we must find the greatest alignment. For if we are connected to the Universal Mind, yet most of our thoughts are not our own, still we are directly responsible for creating physicality. That is a large responsibility for many of us to place our minds around.

So rather than attempting to place everything in the right order, we can seek to fulfil the second definition and find a sense of harmony which is inevitably found at the core of any agreement.

One way we can align our minds is to align our space to resonate and represent the sense of harmony we are seeking. Simply speaking, this means removing anything that is not in harmony.

Shirley's Case Study:

Shirley is a well-rounded woman in her late 40s with a beautiful family, consisting of one teenage son and one twelve-year-old daughter, and of course, her loving and kind husband. They live in a lovely home in the northern suburbs of Sydney.

Shirley was financially successful in the past, having run her own successful recruitment businesses. However, at the time of the consultation she was experiencing a lull in her business mojo and lack of clarity for a clear path moving forward. This included significantly decreased income, which was then creating a flow-on effect, including strain on her loving marriage.

Although she attended several high-quality personal development courses covering a variety of life areas including financial abundance, she felt stuck and was both unmotivated and frustrated about her sense of future abundance.

After some time of listening to Shirley's needs and apparent obstacles, it became evident there was an issue with her space at home contributing to the problem. This was even more evident as the work issues appeared not long after moving to their home some four years ago. This coincided with Shirley closing her previous office space when they moved to the new residence and she was running her home office from the residence.

During the next few hours, we discussed a variety of areas that needed to be addressed ranging from Feng Shui energetic patterning relating to wealth through to clearing techniques, and most of all, Shirley's mind alignment. We agreed on a handful of simple changes, which I left her to implement.

After a few weeks, I rang to touch base to see how Shirley was progressing and was delighted to hear the excitement in her voice. She explained they'd followed all the suggestions I made. She shared the simple changes they experienced as a family and how happy they were all feeling with the improvements. Finally, at the very end of the phone call, Shirley shared that in the month since I visited, she'd generated over $70k of new income easily.

I followed up with Shirley four months later to see how things were progressing, and she again shared that it amazed her at having generated over $200k of income with hardly any effort. Their home transformed into their very own business profitability generator, and all other areas of their life were continuing to blossom.

(The names in this section are fictitious to protect client confidentiality.)

The Reflection/Creation exercise:

Take a piece of paper and a pen and sit in front of a mirror.

Looking at yourself for a full three minutes and reflect on the life you are currently living.

At the completion of the three minutes answer the following questions by circling the quality that is more predominant.

My life currently is having more:
- Peace/Chaos
- Joy/Sadness
- Variety/Monotony
- Adventure/Boredom
- Freedom/Obligations
- Pleasure/Pain
- Abundance/Scarcity
- Connection/Isolation
- Courage/Fear
- Love/Loneliness

Now consider the life you wish to create and choose the top three qualities you wish to experience more of:

I choose to create a life that is filled with:

1)
2)
3)

Now go to your wardrobe, choose one of the following

Your underwear drawer
Your sock drawer
Your shirts

Send the picture to someone you trust and who does not live with you and ask them to answer the same questions you previously answered above:

Thank you for being of service to me: They say you can tell a lot about a person's inner life by the state of their wardrobe. Please choose from the following emotions the quality that is more predominant in this picture:
- Peace/Conflict
- Order/Chaos
- Joy/Sadness
- Variety/Monotony
- Adventure/Boredom
- Freedom/Obligations
- Pleasure/Pain
- Abundance/Scarcity
- Connection/Isolation
- Courage/Fear
- Love/Loneliness

Take a moment to compare the two responses. What are the qualities you and the other person both chose? These will be primary areas that require attention in your life.

What are the qualities the other person chose that you did not? These are secondary areas for you to contemplate. These may be more subtle, or perhaps require further examination. i.e. Scarcity may not be a scarcity of money but a scarcity of time. Take some time to contemplate if there is a subtle or secondary way in which this quality presents in your life.

Now take a moment to recall what were the top three qualities you wished to create more of in your life.

What could this image look like in the future if you were living the life you truly wished to create? Would it have more colour, would it be more organised etc. Decide now what changes you will make to your inner drawer and place a note to yourself in this drawer that can be easily read.

I choose to create a life filled with:

Every day when I dress, I remind myself that I am:

BODY

"There has been a revolution with how we perceive the body. What appears to be a three-dimensional object, an anatomical structure is actually a process, a constant flow of information."
DEEPAK CHOPRA

THE DOORWAY BETWEEN THE PHYSICAL AND SPIRITUAL

What if I was to tell you most of the information they've sold you about the spiritual realm being somewhere beyond this reality was a fallacy?

The idea we need to move beyond something or beyond ourselves to experience spiritual connection is only one way to describe a method to experiencing an awakening.

The fact is, spirituality is everywhere, and it is very much in physical form. We have already discussed that within the physical realm are hidden doorways that contain the secrets to the connections we seek. Almost like The Lion, the Witch and the Wardrobe, as you step into the wardrobe, it transports you to a different place and time, or a different version of space.

I spent most of my life feeling there was something more to

life and not knowing how to get there. The feeling of a proximity so close I could sense and almost smell it, led to years of many frustrated tears. I prayed for the one magical moment when I could finally understand the truth of what enlightenment is.

Perhaps it's maturity, or perhaps its cynicism, or perhaps it's just a healthy dose of wisdom, but to me, these days it has been a culmination of experiences in what is still just a beginning.

I have been blessed with moments in my life of what I can only describe as intense and immediate insights. I believe one of these insights to be a truth. Within the physicality of this world lies the physical evidence of the link between the ordinary and the extraordinary in life.

For many, stepping beyond all of 'what is' is too confronting. May I suggest there is an easier path that is a step-by-step, moment-by-moment, space-by-space journey through life.

We experience life in a physical body which is governed by electrical impulses. We experience life energetically so it's essential to understand the energetics of one's body, including how to maintain it, how to clear it, and how to elevate it. When you have this understanding, it will automatically change the relationship you have to space itself.

Just as spaces need clearing so too, do our bodies. It's ironic that we meticulously brush our teeth once or twice a day, yet we very rarely look after the energetic systems of our bodies. But did you know we have more than one?

Aside from our physical body, we have an emotional body, a mental body and an energetic body. According to Donna Eden in her book, Energy Medicine, we have nine main systems that encompass our body as energy. Meridian, Chakras, Aura, Basic Grid, Celtic Weave, 5 Rhythms, Triple Warmer, Radiant Circuits and the electrics.

Now, I do not profess to see energetic systems visually like Donna does, however, I can attest to having seen energetic fields around people, animals and even vegetation. I have also witnessed the shifting nature of these fields as the physical space around them has been re-energised.

I, too, have had personal experience with practitioners working on my energetic systems and have felt a palpable difference from the effect of their adjustments. The art of acupuncture is one of my favourite modalities focusing on the Meridian System. A few years ago, I suffered a prolapsed disc in my spine and would often find myself unable to walk for days or even weeks at a time.

I recall one event vividly. I was doubled over in intense back pain, barely able to get to the car. I was due to travel overseas to see my daughter, who was in boarding school in the USA at the time. I needed to find a way within twenty-four hours not only to walk again, but travel by plane, and drive several hours at the other end. "This will hurt," the acupuncturist said as he pierced a single point above my lip. Oh boy, was that an understatement. It made the pain from the prolapsed disc pale by comparison. However, after the treatment, not only I could walk again, I could fly the next day lifting my suitcase along the way too.

Our bodies are vibrating particles of energy, so it really is our choice if we want that energy to be clear and bright, or dense and dark. When heavy energy affects us, it will naturally be much harder to see life from a clear perspective. Doing things to cleanse and clear our energy is vital for one's clarity whether that be by looking at the food and nutrients we eat, or the water we drink. Or whether it's the way we clear and connect with our Chakras and other energy systems. It all forms the foundation of our experience in a body.

This concept is at the very centre of our gateway to spirituality.

As humans, we seek to understand through realisation how the physical realms and the energetic realms connect. Like a swinging saloon door, the irony is the door is not closed to either side. Imagine the dramatic scene in a movie where the heroine pushes the hidden book in the bookcase and suddenly it spins around to reveal a hidden room. In actuality, we are living in this crossover complexity of energies all the time. It's just that we perhaps see it only from the perspective of the side of the doorway from which we currently perceive.

For those of us on the planet who can sense things beyond the norm, it can sometimes be a confusing place to be with far too few people to share it with. For many years in my life I kept my experiences very close to my chest for fear of judgement and perhaps even ridicule. Those who are clairvisual, clairvoyant or clairaudient will at some time share our stories about how we came to understand what the heck was happening. As an opening occurs, and the extrasensory perception expands, it takes some time to integrate, especially when it's not usually something others find relatable.

I wish I had someone in my early 20s who could have explained to me in basic English what I was experiencing. It would've made the next twenty years a lot less challenging. So, all things start within the body and how the body exchanges energy within the physical spaces we occupy. Naturally, we will gravitate to places that uplift our sense of spirit, however there are also places we should avoid.

Just as Masaru Emoto demonstrated music could change the crystalline structure of water, our bodies are composed of over 60% water, and in some organs, up to 84%. It follows suit then that our bodies are also influenced on a cellular level by the vibrations of our surroundings. The energetic charge of a physical space will have a direct relationship on our bodies and also the sense we have of our own energetic connection. A harmonious space encourages a harmonious connection as an example.

It is a great myth that spirituality or enlightenment is something beyond us. In my view, it is better described as the very essence of who we are. The essence or natural way of feeling connected to one's understanding of life (oneself), while walking with your feet firmly planted on the ground can be a tad challenging. I mean, who hasn't found themselves at times when we would rather live in an alternate space than the current place we find ourselves in? This juxtaposition of mastering several realms at the same time is really what life is all about. It has been an enormous comfort knowing that at any time, the gateway is an internal doorway available to be opened to an experience of the beyond.

Everywhere we look around, time will indicate that we are operating within several spaces at the same time. In the same way we have a mind with no mind, and we have a body with no body.

I was very fortunate with the birth of my first child to be introduced to an amazing yogi master (well before downward dog was trendy, mind you). A beautiful woman named Cate amazed me as she explained the only reason we feel pain in the human body is if it connects to our physical body through the breath. Without breath in our bodies, we feel no pain, as is often the case when we naturally change our breathing in the event of trauma. Under normal circumstances, with an extended period of time without breath, we would be dead. So, we set about practising the lion's breath circulating prana in through alternating nostrils and holding all the breath out for what felt like an eternity. I was flooded with the intensity of past memories of being forcibly drowned.

Facing the fear of not having breath in my body was luckily

less than my desire to create new life easily. So I continued to practise and practise until I knew I would not die if there was no breath in my lungs for a regulated time. That my spirit was well and truly alive even if I did not breathe for an extra few seconds.

The time arrived to give birth, and with every contraction that arrived, I exhaled the air from my body, holding no breath whatsoever, mirroring the timing of the impending pain. Maintaining myself in a state of calmness knowing I could control the experience was the most challenging part. Nothing to do with physicality, solely managing my mind. This continued over many hours, during which time I felt no pain.

Somewhat of a personal story to share at this point in the book, but the relevance is it demonstrated to me that not everything is as it seems. Often it only presents as it seems, because that's what they've led us to believe. There is a lot more happening on this planet than we understand.

Humankind loves complexity and yet yearns for simplicity. I know often in my life I've made many things much, much more difficult than needed so I could experience the thrill and drama of overcoming enormous difficulty. This complexity was a giant distraction and in hindsight, held me back from experiencing the raw enlightened understanding I so desperately was seeking. Inevitably, I have found it to be something that arrives through experience, finding language to convey that experience is often an even bigger challenge. It's like going to France and having somebody speak Italian to you. You don't speak the same language, so whilst you cannot translate the actual words, there is an experiential understanding in the communication.

What will happen uniquely for each person at the perfect point in time depends on their intention, and the commitment each of us bring to the realisation of that intention. And there are also many who are not concerned with seeking this intention. This is also fine for each of us are here in our own way, in our own time, living life as we choose it to be in parallel to indications there is something far greater going on.

JOANNA JAMES

"We shape our buildings thereafter they shape us."
WINSTON CHURCHILL

PHYSICAL SPACE AND YOUR HEALTH

Now we come to the part where we talk about those things that are scientifically measurable. That's because there are many people on the planet who do not understand the onslaught of toxicity we are expecting our physical bodies to integrate every day, from a multiplicity of sources.

By a blessing, an event of fate connected me to the study of Building Biology, a discipline that grew after the Second World War because of sick building syndrome discovered in the post-war housing complexes. Sick building syndrome is exactly as it reads—buildings that make the occupants sick!

With the event of modern construction post the oil crisis of the 70s, buildings were constructed to be extra airtight, with a reduced airflow and often reliant on mechanical ventilation. As a result, there was evidenced a link to an extraordinarily high level of illness in the occupants. Common symptoms are often general and non-descript including headache, dizziness, nausea, skin irritation, mental fatigue, difficulty concentrating, and irritation of the eyes, nose, and throat.

Building biology involves identifying and dealing with the health hazards in the home from allergens like mould, to manmade chemicals and electromagnetic fields. Designers who are creating spaces, or as BB practitioners who are called in to investigate why a building might contribute to health concerns, can utilise this.

I recall, humorously, the decisive grin of my amazing teacher, Nicole Bijlsma, who said, "You can't *un-know* what you now know." Little did I realise how true this would be and how deep the horror would run. I realised that for many years of my architectural practice, I'd been inadvertently exposing my clients to the effects of manmade chemicals and manmade electromagnetic fields that may have been potentially harmful over time. As the shock wore off, I replaced it with a sense of outrage that I could have completed such a long graduate degree of six years without any basic knowledge of Building Biology whatsoever.

In the following years, through an understanding of the principles of Building biology, it has guided me to learn how the physical space we live in has a direct relationship to our health.

Knowing each person has a different genetic blueprint that naturally translates into different health strengths and different health weaknesses, it is impossible to say for sure that one thing has specifically caused a specific health event. However, it has been scientifically evidenced and documented repeatedly now that there are buildings that make people sick. So there are many things within our built environment which we are yet to fully understand to educate the wider population.

I can hear you asking, "So where do I start?"

As is with the rest of life, the physical spaces we live in are complex environments with many things happening all at the same time. There is a significant body of evidence demonstrating correlations between health hazards like air and drinking water quality, and VOCs *(Volatile Organic Compounds)* gassing from new construction materials, to adverse human health outcomes. Add to this, the sea of electropollution that now bathes the entire planet arising from our addiction to wireless technologies and cell phones, let alone the rollout of the infrastructure required to support the fifth generation (5G) of mobile telecommunications.

I can visualise a future version of David Attenborough delivering an opening address at the United Nations. Here, he'll explain in his distinguished British candour that we are facing yet another manmade disaster on a global scale. Detailed support of this speech would be even more extensive scientific research regarding the detrimental health effects of electromagnetic fields, exposure to chemicals, mould toxicity, water and air contaminants.

MOULD

My experience conducting assessments shows that when you overlay and map the patterns of the findings, that the diagrammatic depiction of the exposure matches *the adverse effect on people's health.* While it's often sought after in cheese, mould is not a sexy topic to discuss. However, there will come a time soon when the discussions about biotoxins that reside in water-damaged buildings will become mainstream as evidenced by the recent Parliamentary Inquiry on Biotoxin Illness in 2018.

Water damage can occur in a building for many reasons, and not necessarily from a natural disaster flood event. Everyday events such as an overflowing bathtub, broken tap or flexible hosing, degraded waterproof membranes that have lost their integrity. Other causes may arise from poorly designed buildings that encourage the build-up of condensation, exposure to moisture during construction, following a flood event or simply by living in a humid climate. Damage can even occur from excess water vapours created by occupants such as not turning the exhaust fan on when bathing.

When a material is exposed to water for forty-eight hours or more without being dried, it creates the perfect environment for the growth of biotoxins like fungi and bacteria and their by-products. (Mycotoxins, microbial volatile organic compounds and endotoxins).

Adverse health effects arising from exposure to a water-damaged building.

Despite many well-researched papers linking a long list of negative health effects to dampness in buildings, there are currently no legally enforceable standards in Australia for exposure to biotoxins in water-damaged buildings. There are also many scientific reviews that have considered the adverse health effects from exposure to dampness or (WDB) that demonstrate the following acute symptoms can occur within a matter of hours or days. These can be flu-like symptoms, headaches, fever, cough, exacerbation of asthma and hypersensitivity pneumonitis. Other documented symptoms may include respiratory and asthma-related health concerns, bronchitis, wheeze asthma, night dry cough, morning cough, sensitivity to inhaled allergens, and hay fever.

What is even more staggering is approximately 24% of the world's population have a genetic disposition which means their acquired immune response does not recognise the foreign toxins and so will not create antigens which in turn makes them susceptible to chronic inflammation. The effect of this inflammation is a depletion in key neurotransmitters such as MSH (Melanocyte-Stimulating Hormone) and VIP (Vasoactive Intestinal Polypeptide) which results in sleep disturbances, fibromyalgia, candida and an increase in other bacterial infections.

Other symptoms of Biotoxin illness can include fatigue often presenting as chronic fatigue like symptoms and brain fog, including short-term memory loss. These are often misdiagnosed as being Lyme's disease. Understanding this puts a new perspective on things, and I am sure the day will come to stimulate changes in the way the medical industry diagnoses patients moving forward.

Children are particularly susceptible as are the elderly, or any person with an already compromised immune system, is more likely to be at risk from exposure.

What is often more alarming than understanding the full health effects of something as simple as mould, is the lack of understanding surrounding it. To put things into perspective, the health effects may occur without any visible evidence. Often there can be a chemical stew festering inside the walls, insulation, cupboards and cavities of a building. A visual Contrast Sensitivity (VCS) test, whilst not a diagnostic tool, is a good screening tool to indicate if it has affected a person. They also use this test for patients who have been exposed to chemicals and solvents as it shows damage to the optic nerves. I suggest that all household members complete a free screening tool: **https://www.vcstest.com/register/**

For more general references on Mould and Dampness in buildings please see page 84

ELECTROMAGNETIC FIELDS

This was by far my favourite subtopic. Especially of note was the delight of the few gentlemen in the course who demonstrated pure joy when we fired up our meters to measure the invisible. Apparently, boys love toys.

So what is an Electromagnetic Field anyway?

In simple terms, we are exposed to four different types of EMFs (JOHNSON, 2017)

1. **Radiofrequency radiation (RF)** from Wi-Fi enabled devices such as smart meters, mobile and cordless phones, appliances (printers, baby monitors, speakers, smart TVs etc), antennas and towers, and broadcast transmission towers.
2. **Extra low frequency AC magnetic fields (EMF)** are generated by current emitted from appliances such as an oven, fridge motor or smart meter, and overhead power lines.
3. **Extra Low Frequency AC electric fields** are generated from voltage emitted from electrical wiring, and appliances connected to power.
4. **Dirty Electricity (DE)** also known as dirty mains, dirty power, or electrical pollution, describes the problem of electromagnetic noise on the mains wiring of a house.

Current Exposure Standards in Australia

Australia's standards for EMF and RF are based on the International Commission for Non-Ionising Radiation Protection (ICNIRP) which evaluates the short-term effects of heating tissue (RF) and induced electric currents on the body (AC MF). We base both on the premise of a healthy 100 kg male and do not take into consideration effects on a child or a developing foetus.

Not surprisingly, the development of exposure standards in Australia is not without a controversial past of concealment, and perhaps consultation and coercion with the telecommunication industry. We base the current standards for RF on information formulated in 1998 which fails to differentiate between a continuous waved device such as AM/FM radios and a pulsed signal such as WIFI signals. Additionally, Australian Standards do not address a long-term exposure to sources of EMF and RF, which is now so obviously the case in modern day life.

Australia is not the only country governed by outdated regulations. The 2012 Bio Initiative Report explained the key areas pertaining to the proven health risks associated with these types of exposures at levels well below commonly used international standards. This report is evidence-based and is independent of governments, existing bodies and industry professional societies that refer to outdated and inadequate standards.

In the Summary given by Cindy Sage MA, she explains, "Human beings are bioelectrical systems. Human hearts and brains are regulated by internal bioelectrical signals and as such environmental exposures to artificial EMFs can interact with fundamental biological processes in the human body."

Sage explains current exposure limits for telecommunications are based on the presumption that heating of tissue (for RF) or induced electric currents in the body (for ELF) are the only concern. Hence we base exposure standards on the flawed assumption that this is the right way to measure how much non-ionising energy a human can tolerate. However, it is now proven that adverse health effects occur at much lower levels of exposure where no heating occurs at all.

EMF Effects

According to Deanne Alban's article, "Alarming ways that EMF are affecting your brain," some the reported effects of EMF are headaches, dizziness, sleep disorders, benign tumours, and dementia." We have connected exposure to EMF with changes in the nervous system and brain function such as Alzheimer's Disease, Motor Neuron Disease and Parkinson's Disease. Ahlbom explains the role of the blood-brain barrier is a group of specialised cells that acts as a filter to keep the brain safe from toxins, heavy metals, pathogens, drugs, and other foreign substances. Exposure to EMFs increases permeability of the blood-brain barrier, compromising it, and allowing chemicals like mercury, aluminium and viruses to easily enter the brain (NITTBY et al. 2008).

Long-term exposure to EMFs can also affect proteins in the brain and interfere with the levels of serotonin, dopamine, and norepinephrine causing adverse effects on mood, memory, learning, and stress. (FRAGOPOULOU et al. 2012) https://www.ncbi.nlm.nih.gov/pubmed/22263702

When cells are under attack from environmental toxins or adverse conditions, there is a special protection launched by the body. This stress response releases stress proteins to help survive in certain situations such as high temperatures, lack of oxygen, heavy metals, and oxidative stress. ELF and RF exposures can now add to this list of environmental factors that generate this response. (ACES 2016)

Long-term EMF exposure creates free radicals that are unattached oxygen molecules which attack cells much in the same way that metal rusts. The brain is highly vulnerable to free radical damage in the form of both ageing and cell damage. (SIMKO, M & MATTSSON, MO, 2004)

Ahlbom also explains brain cells communicate with each other via chemicals known as neurotransmitters. Neurotransmitters regulate mood, sleep, motivation, ability to learn, addictions, and more. Long-term exposure to EMFs can interfere with levels of serotonin, dopamine, and norepinephrine causing adverse effects on mood, memory, learning, and stress.

EMF AND CANCERS

If the list of general effects above is not enough to prick your interest or turn your tummy, then perhaps the long list of even more serious conditions may. According to the BioInitiative Report, much lower levels of acceptable (legal) EMF are linked to childhood leukemia, other cancers in both children and adults, and brain tumours. They can directly relate the risks of cancer to damaged DNA, for when genes are damaged, they produce damaged cells. When damaged cells continue to reproduce themselves, this is one of the pre-conditions for cancer.

BRAIN TUMOURS

I often laugh when the telecommunication companies send out a text message to all their network stating they have advised you of potential health hazards of using their products. One can see forward into the future when legal court cases abound, not too dissimilar to the previous turn against the Marlboro man in the 70s.

It was over five years ago that Telstra started regularly sending all users the advice from the World Health Organisation (WHO) about how to "reduce mobile phone exposure." Conveniently, they omitted the WHO also stated in its finding that radio frequency electromagnetic energy emitted from mobiles was "possibly carcinogenic to humans."

They recommend to owners:
1. Use hands-free devices to keep mobile phones away from the head and body during phone calls.
2. Limit the number and length of calls.
3. Use the phone in areas of good reception to reduce exposure as the phone will transmit at reduced power.

This would seem to pair nicely with recent evidence that there is a two time increase in risk when using a mobile phone for over ten years. **https://www.ncbi.nlm.nih.gov/pubmed/19328536**

As someone who racks up lengthy talk time on the mobile phone for work, I am often confronted by how best to manage things moving forward. Often, I am perceived as the weird one who places my phone on the boardroom table with a very, very long headset cord in tow. Perhaps it's the high-pitched squeal I can hear through my high-frequency metre. Or it's the knowing I wake up with a blinding headache whenever my phone is not on aeroplane mode or an unexpected modem is nearby.

One thing is for sure, I struggle to watch all the innocent ones with their mobile phones tucked neatly in their chest or jeans pockets. I draw the line when I come across women tucking their phones into their bras for convenience and inevitably cannot hold back expressing genuine concern for their safety.

What is even more disturbing is the number of other sources inside a home that emit similar signals having effects on the unknowing occupants. So whilst I could fill another thirty pages with commentary on the different effects that EMF may contribute to, and the scientific papers that say they do, there is one of particular noteworthy of mention.

For general references on EMF please refer to page 84

HYPERSENSITIVITY

Electrical Hypersensitivity

(EHS) is estimated to affect approximately 3-5% of the population.

According to Bevington (2013) and the British Society of Ecological Medicine (2014) symptoms can include headache, fatigue, stress, sleep disturbances, skin prickling, burning sensations and rashes, heart palpitations, tinnitus, pain and ache in muscles and many other health problems.

In April 2009, the European Parliament (April 2012) submitted a Written Declaration to the World Health Organisation stating that EHS should be declared a medical condition in its own right.

An increasing number of people have now been diagnosed with EHS Electromagnetic Hypersensitivity.

According to a survey by Yasuko Kato, Prof. Olle Johansson An in 2012, many of the subjects suffered symptoms so severely they couldn't maintain their employment because of the environmental conditions. Therefore they suffered health, economic and social impacts. (IEMFA, 2017) **http://www.iemfa.org/publications/**

For general references on Electromagnetic Hypersensitivity please see page 85

Perhaps it's the Finance GM in me emerging, however, there really is nothing like the numbers. They speak for themselves. Below is a chart showing the vast difference between what are recommended levels and what are actual levels of acceptable exposure.

As seen below, Australia has current safety standards that are well in excess of many countries around the world. The current ARPANSA exposure limits can vary up to one million times greater than the recommended limits.

Comparison Charts between standards:

Radio Frequencies found in Nature -0.000001 **uW/m²**

HOW AUSTRALIA COMPARES TO OTHER COUNTRIES

Australia	Up to 10 million uW/m²
Bulgaria, Italy, India, Israel, France, Poland & Russia	100,000
China	60,000
Switzerland	40,000
Luxembourg	20,000
Salzburg Resolution (2000)	10,000
Salzburg, Austria Outside	10
Inside	1
BioInitiative Report 2012	3 to 6
Seletun Statement	170

SBM - 2008 BUILDING BIOLOGY GUIDELINES

Extreme concern	Severe concern	Slight concern	No concern
>1,000 uW/m²	10-1,000 uW/m²	0.1 - 10 uW/m²	< 0.1 uW/m²

So, I watch with bated breath as the new 5G network is being rolled out across the nation and the documentaries and community protests swell. As they say only time will tell, I hope not too many people suffer unnecessarily in the meantime; myself included.

BUILDING MATERIALS

Having felt such a deep resonance with the new reality of things in 2012, I decided to create a bio home. Renovated using the principles of Building Biology, I learned as much as I could to create a finished product with zero fields. I would stay awake in the wee hours of the morning trying to research the best products to use. However, rapidly the stone-cold reality dawned on me that despite the very best of product selection, most products are fixed using a spectrum of toxic glues. After many phone calls to major adhesive manufacturers, people asked who I was and why I was asking for SDS (Safety Data sheets) and other data that most people including architects did not. "What are you intending to use this information for?" They would ask, to which I would respond, "To build the safest home I can for my family, of course."

Sometimes after trying more natural adhesives, there came a point when I needed to take the middle line and accept all building involves toxicity vs wearability. Each person must draw their own set of conclusions and standards. As with all things, it's an individual choice we each hold relative to our own set of beliefs we hold around the subject matter. There is no right or wrong, only degrees of understanding and knowledge. As we move forward into a new future, I trust that one day we will uncover the true level of exposure we live by day to day and we can make empowered choices collectively.

Mould and EMF are but just a few areas to consider within spaces, whether it be contaminants in the air or in water, or chemicals from the cleaning products that many people have in their cupboards. You can see the direct effect that it has on the health of so many. A few staggering statistics to consider from the book, *Healthy Home Healthy Family* by Nicole Bijlsma before we leave this chapter of the book are:

- 1 in 3 children will experience allergies by the age of 5.
- People with allergies have a 5 to 13-fold increased risk for being chemically sensitive.
- Living within two hundred metres of a major road was associated with an increased risk of asthma and allergic outcomes in susceptible individuals.
- There are over 140 million chemicals registered for use on the world's largest database. The Chemical Abstracts Service and most of the manmade portion of these chemicals have never been assessed for their impact on human health.
- Incense smoke produces 4.5 times more particulates than cigarette smoke.
- Over 5000 different chemicals are used in hair dye products, some of which are reported to be carcinogenic in animals.
- The largest study ever conducted on fluoride, identified a significant decline in children's IQ later in life if exposure to fluoride occurred in the womb.
- Boiling water does little more than kill bacteria that can't survive at 100 degrees Celsius and evaporate chlorine from the water. It does very little to improve water quality.

- Attached garages can significantly elevate the indoor concentrations to toxic particles and gases such as carbon monoxide, formaldehyde, naphthalene and other carcinogens.
- Homes built on a concrete slab or apartments constructed using concrete masonry may take months or years to cure. Each cubic metre of concrete will release around ninety litres of moisture into the indoor air, raising the humidity.

https://www.buildingbiology.com.au/Biology/healthy-home-healthy-family.html

JOANNA JAMES

> *"Our relationship lives in*
> *the space between us which is sacred."*
> MARTIN BUBER

SPACE AND YOUR RELATIONSHIPS

Life is dualistic in nature. When we review the Law of Gender, there is always a yin and yang. Not surprisingly, we too are made of both yin and yang energies, and we can command the quantities of both energies. It has taken me many years to embrace both the male and female energies that flow through my being. Just like driving a car and shifting gears, I can see now I have varying degrees of intensity, in a variety of situations depending on my focus and response to external stimuli. This dynamic has had a profound effect on my relating space and It will continue to do so moving forward.

As if the duality within myself is not enough to master, the physical space and how it affects your relationships is a complicated and often underestimated thing. Most of us would agree we've all had our fair share of easy-going and challenging relationships, and that this is one mechanisms by which humans learn and grow. It's confronting to imagine that a physical space can affect our relationships. Yet when we select a space to live or work in, we are attracted to that space and it becomes one of our life's teachers in a unique and purposeful way.

Revisiting the universal law that like attracts like, one can describe there will be a resonance in the energetic patterning of a space. This may indicate the likely outcomes for the relationships occurring within the container. This may vary room by room and person by person depending on one's awareness, commitment and resolve. Sometimes it can be the amount of stress people are experiencing from living in spaces and not understanding how the spaces are affecting them, often placing unknowingly great strain on their relationships.

There is nothing more difficult in a relationship than when one person is unwell or suffering, be that emotionally, mentally or physically. Feeling on edge within a physical space can affect the dynamics of a relationship. It can often take some time to understand the subtlety of how a physical space is directly impacting our energetics.

The first step to having healthy relationships is to hold a healthy relationship with the spaces we live in. This requires a component of responsibility or ownership in how we primarily care and relate to ourselves. This factor is magnified or diminished by our willingness to accept, engage and acknowledge our own process of creation.

I have received this lesson many times, however, none more challenging than that of my twenty-year marriage separation. Having set about to create a home I thought was perfectly balanced, it was not until sometime after the event I retraced my learnings. I recognised the uncanny combination of untreated and excessive geopathic stress generated by the oceanfront location, combined with my intense focus during the renovations to enhance and change the previous energetic charts. Essentially,

I had accidently, yet purposefully created a new paradigm of an entirely different potentiality. This is not to say that I did not have personal accountability for the destruction of my marriage, for I absolutely did. With hindsight, the course of events potentially could be altered if I understood earlier the full extent of that likely occurrence, and the predictive power of the energetics I was creating within. Sharing this many years later still brings a teary eye, and equally the desire to help others, so they may be empowered to choose futures more consciously than I did at that time.

Often, we search for reasons and understanding after experiencing a life-changing event. For me, there was a significant *aha* moment when finally, I could see a larger picture was also in play.

On a light-hearted note, perhaps the new stepping stone for all of those women dating may be more poignant to ask, "What does the energetic chart of your home show with respect to love and abundance?" Not, "What is their relationship like with their mother?" And as often the case when people live together, there is a shift into a new physical space whether that be for either or both parties. This is also a moment to realise energetic shifts occur for the new occupant within the dynamic of the relationship. Or the relationship itself is shifting to a new energetic experience when both parties move into a new home. Understanding what the effect of the space has on the evolution of your relationship is essential to understand.

This seems to be the moment to discuss the Universal Law of Perpetual Transmutation, namely that all things are in a state of constant change. So often in relationships, we seek change either in the other person or a change of feeling within oneself, and yet we often also seek security or no change at all. For us to truly embrace the only thing that is constant in the universe is change can be a mind warp as we view the physicality of life as finite within time.

Perhaps the solution to this is to consider the Law of Compensation when considering relationships being that we receive what we give. With all relationships, whether they be romantic or otherwise, our experience is a direct reflection of what we emit. In this way, we too may play with the physical spaces we hold relationships within, giving to those spaces the qualities with which we enhance our relationships. Not too dissimilar to a blossoming flower, a space is can receive energy, and the space will emit that energy in return.

In this way, it is possible to supercharge a space to become a generator of love, peace, tranquillity, vibrance and any other quality we wish to experience in our relationship worlds.

Equally, without a thorough understanding of this, a space may become a reflection of loneliness, frustration, anger or sadness. The more we magnify this, the more it progresses, and so the loop goes on and on until that particular cycle is disrupted.

As you can see, this extends far beyond entry level Feng Shui's description of the 'romance corner' of a bedroom. How we create in a relationship that is unfolding is something worth considering. To participate in creating a space that is clear and balanced, supportive, loving and in harmony will help to contribute to the basis of a blossoming relationship.

"Clutter is not just physical stuff. It's old ideas, toxic relationships and bad habits. Clutter is anything that does not support your best self."
ELEANOR BROWNN

CLEARING YOUR ENERGY

And so, we've talked a lot in this section of the book about the body as it relates to physical spaces. It is time to come back to simple practices that can be put into action to promote optimal opportunity in your life.

Learning how to clear your body, on all levels including physical, mental, emotional and energetic levels is as unique as we are individuals. There are plenty of practices that will hold varying levels of effectiveness for each individual, also relative to the degree to which we practise them.

From my experience, there is no one way and so the important thing to realise is to try various things until you find what works for you. Below are some of my ideas on things that have worked for me in my life experience:

Physical: Fasting including juice fasting, spending time in nature, particularly barefoot or in a way that's earthing. Drinking more pure water, obtaining the correct amount of sunlight, spending time in water (both hot and cold). Eating more nourishing foods or those foods that help to detoxify the body's systems, even bouts of raw foods and plant-based foods only. Saunas, steam rooms and hot pools—I love hot springs, especially those charged with minerals such as silica. Magnesium baths, essential oils, scrubs and clays to extract toxins. Enemas. Colonic hydration. Exercise of all kinds, from gentle yin yoga to weights to aerobic workouts.

Mentally: Writing out lists, talking things through, meditating, practising mindfulness, listening to relaxation music, sitting still and sometimes doing nothing. Listening to new patterns of interesting ideas to replace stagnant ones. Observing the various voices of the mind and enquiring about the physical experiences of the body as it relates to ideas and meanings. Vibrational treatments such as sound healings.

Emotional: Crying and laughing either together or separately as needed. Healthy expression of anger in a controlled environment—punching a boxing bag with intent, hitting a pillow with a bat, smashing old plates. Writing down feelings, then burning the paper to release them. Naming and owning the various emotions, speaking from my heart when I share them with others, talking with friends, or professional support about what my feelings are, hugs and physically being held. Consciously choosing to express joy, love and gratitude whenever I can. Allowing emotions to move through me.

Energetic: Exercises to clear my chakras, grounding and releasing energetic influences, attachments or old energetic patterns. Practising release and forgiveness techniques such as

Ho'oponopono, Kundalini bioenergetic shaking, Sufi spinning, visiting power places and sacred sites, calling on vibrational being for support and assistance.

In a similar way that we require a variety of all the above to maintain optimal health, so, too, do spaces. Whilst is it commonly accepted the benefit of physically cleaning a space helps, rarely are we shown how to cleanse and clear spaces in other ways.

The following are simple exercises that can be done as standalone exercises or done in combination. It is most potent when done in sequence and with regularity.

1. Remove any clutter, broken objects or objects in disrepair that are no longer needed or hold negative meaning. The physical removal of objects creates a vacuum for new energy to rush into.
2. Cleanse the entire space with sage or other energetic spritzers such as Paolo Santo with all doors and windows open which allows the Chi (energy) to move. Any sound that feels appropriate also helps to make energy move.
3. Clean things that support the objects such as shelves, buffets or house goods. Remove all dirt and debris. Use nontoxic cleaning products such as Abode cleaning products. **https://www.shopnaturally.com.au/brands/abode-cleaning/**
4. Place within the environment objects that remind you of the life you intend to create. The mind works on subconscious repetition, so the more objects you can place with significant meaning, the more anchors you will have within the home. I like to create within one room of the house a special place as an offering of intention. Imagine a 3-dimensional vision board and you are on the right track.

5. Acknowledge the space and seal its energy. Sometimes it helps to call in any other energies you stand guard by your door. This can be generic or specific and has no limitation beyond what is desirable to you. I like to imagine a giant invisible box encapsulating the entire property.

We brush our teeth daily, yet most people never clear their space. I feel for those who move into new homes or new apartments. They don't understand the energetic soup they have just walked into and the years and years of history that has been captured within the walls of the home. Some space cleansings are ordinary, and some are extraordinary. After all, everything has its place.

For simplicity's sake, a good space clearing routine is not too dissimilar to how we wash our clothes or change our sheets and can be a wonderful ritual to practice with friends or family. When my children were younger, they loved to follow me as I cleared our home with small bells chiming.

Learning to clear and look after your physical body and your physical spaces is just as important as understanding what is happening to them. It is an ongoing process that requires commitment to maintain.

For those who travel frequently, as you move through hotel rooms and other spaces, it is very handy to understand how to clear that space quickly so it can be conducive and support you while you rest.

To make sure you can give yourself the best opportunity for a healthy and clear energetic system, it is prudent to learn how to cleanse and take care of yourself as fast as necessary.

Looking after the spaces you live in doesn't have to be complicated. It's a very simple process. It just requires a clear intent and a dedication to the outcome.

Learning how to clear is one of the most important things you can do in life, yet it is something few people teach. It should be something we learn in kindergarten; it is that easy and fun to do.

Roger's Case study:

I was recently blessed with the opportunity to assist a man Roger (alias) who'd gone through a very turbulent breakup. His sister asked me if I could assist with shifting the negativity she'd observed since Roger separated from his partner.

When I arrived at the home, I could sense straight away there was a residual layer of the previous events that occurred within the space which needed to be cleared. The air felt heavy, almost with a dampness to the emotional space that felt like a never ending well of tears and sadness.

As I entered the home, I sensed a white spirit dashing past me, almost like a silver fox or cat passing me by. Whilst it was not in this realm, it made its presence known. I asked Roger if there was a white cat on the property. He seemed bewildered by my question.

As we sat and had a cup of tea, it became obvious Roger was suffering the effects of trauma as there had been abuse, both verbal and physical violence in the home.

There had been several significant events involving excessive drinking and all the energetics attached to that level of consciousness. We talked at length about what Rodger felt he wanted to banish from the home and the life he wanted to create.

As we walked through the space, it became evident to me there were objects that needed to be removed. They held energetic patterning that was not in alignment with the new vision Roger held for his future.

After sharing a cathartic discussion where Roger recounted his experience of pain, suffering and sadness, the emotions were palpable as we moved throughout the house. We talked about his accountability and future responsibility as I explained I would assist him and show him how to undergo the process in the future for himself. Together we moved through the practices.

In essence, it comes down to one thing, intention. Your intention must be clear, intention is everything.

(The names in this section are fictitious to protect client confidentiality.)

Release and Invoke Exercise:

- Gather two pieces of paper and a pen.
- Identify a special place within your home, a sacred corner where you can create an altar or an offering place to yourself where others in the home won't disturb you.
- Find a quiet space to be alone and take ten minutes to really ponder what are three things, emotions, feelings, or experiences you wish to banish from your life. This could be anger, sadness, frustration, or ill health, etc.
- Write them down on the first piece of paper. When you are clear about what you want to remove, find three physical objects in your home that remind or embody what it is you wish to remove.
- Take these objects outside your home and place them in a rubbish removal container. Burn the piece of paper listing them and see their energy disappearing from your life.
- Return to your quiet space and take ten minutes to ponder what are three things, emotions, feelings, or experiences you wish to call into your life. This could be more love, happiness, peace or abundance.
- Choose three objects that resonate with the three things you wish to call forward and place them on your altar alongside your note declaring that:
  I call into my life and home...
- For the next seven days, visit this space every morning when you rise and every night before you retire. Read out the note three times aloud each time, visualising your life with these qualities, objects, emotions in place.

SPACES

Most people think of energy as being electricity or something that travels through wires. The scientific explanation by Anne Helmenstine PhD explains there are ten forms of energy: Mechanical Energy, Thermal Energy, Nuclear Energy, Chemical Energy, Electromagnetic Energy, Sonic Energy, Gravitational Energy, Kinetic Energy, Potential Energy and Ionisation Energy.

We might also agree we can measure energy in alternate ways, perhaps as physical energy, mental energy, or even emotional energy.

Some might say that energy is life or love or even the universe itself or God.

"If you want to find the secret to the universe, think in terms of energy, frequency and vibration."

NICOLA TESLA

SO EXACTLY WHAT IS ENERGY?

Rather than entering an existential versus scientific debate, perhaps what is easier to answer is, "What is the relationship of energy to you?" If each of us received a blue book at birth with the exact prescribed answer, then we would surely be set for life. Ironically, this seems to be one of life's pursuits we all encounter as a truly personalised learning that can only be answered individually. As we move through life, we become more aware of how different energies affect us. We notice the times when we feel energised, the times when we feel depleted and the combination of things in life that vary the impact. Whether it's food, sleep, light or those things not visible at all, most of the time many of us think of energy as being something outside ourselves.

What if we were to find the key to energy is within ourselves and we could dial that energy up and down at will? What would happen if we knew we hold the potential to clarify, to purify, to amplify, and even to broadcast it? If you have an opportunity to read spiritual texts such as 'The Ancient Secrets of the Flower of Life' by Drunvalo

Melchizedek, you will learn about the 'Merkaba' light body. What is a light body, I hear you say?

Diane Ruth Shewmaker explains your light body is a gridwork of light and sacred geometry that brings together your physical, emotional, mental and spiritual being. This body radiates light energy and electromagnetically links your multidimensional self with the infinite universe. The sacred geometry of the light body is also called the "Merkaba". The word Merkaba is both Egyptian and Hebrew for 'a spinning field of light'. It originates from the first eight cells of the fertilised ovum or zygote, and is located at the base of the human spine. Known as the star of David or double tetrahedron, it is from here upon which they build all sacred geometric forms. Humorously, I don't recall my first-year architectural tutor's explanation of the five Platonic solids in any reference to an energy field of geometric forms which when fully expanded is over sixty feet wide.

I have often wondered if the reason I feel so tired at shopping malls is not because of the oppressive, artificial lighting, or monotonous repetition of exactly the same international brands. Perhaps it's because of the combined effect of walking through so many people's energetic fields. It's the realisation that every time you're in a busy public space you are experiencing an energetic soup whether you have physical contact, or have a relationship with a person. The fact is, we are moving balls of energy intertwining every day with a lot of other people's balls of energy.

So how does one manage, measure, protect and nurture one's own energy given that there are many beings in the world?

We would all agree there are places that naturally enhance our energy. Usually they are places in nature that have a clear, vibrant sense of life and vitality about them. When we connect with the energy that renews and reinvigorates our own energy; we find we hold the golden key within. We hold the mastery of our own energy. We hold the ability to protect, to enhance and to secure our own energy. And we also hold the ability to absorb, to soak in, to take and to pilfer other people's energy or that of places and spaces themselves. So once again, with all things in life, it's about responsibility. How do we learn to become responsible for our energy and the energy we maintain? How do we nurture our own energy to continue to grow and support the energies of others?

To understand the unique relationship with one's own energy and how to express one's energy in this world, I'll use a simple example.

When you meet someone new, you simply know. That is, you just like them. Often people say he/she has a nice energy. It's not necessarily something that is rationalised or reasoned as you feel yourself drawn to someone for no other reason than you enjoy being in their field of energy.

Learning about energy, understanding what it is, understanding what it is not, helps clarify what is your energy and what is the energy of others. Once this baseline is established, you have a platform to restore and rejuvenate your energetic field.

This is probably the most essential thing anyone on this planet can learn, yet we seldom teach it in schools other than those of the metaphysical variety. Our emotions impact our energy too. When we are feeling sad and blue or when we are lacking motivation, our energies reflect that state of feeling. When we are feeling happy, bright and vibrant, our energies reflect that state of being too. Managing your energetic state is a second-by-second ongoing thing and similar to lifting weights in a gym, there are exercises that can be done to strengthen our energies too. Understanding the situations that will challenge you and how to prepare for them is an essential part of one's day—just like packing a lunch box is too.

"Your energy is always your first impression. It is the foremost perception others will have of you. This initial energy introduction is a calling card you cannot fake."
ANTHON ST MAARTEN

MAPPING YOUR ENERGY SIGNATURE

The Law of Vibration states everything is in motion and has a unique energy signature.

Mapping your energy signature isn't an art. It may seem impossible to plot or create a diagram of something invisible to the naked eye, however it can be understood as your unique energy signature. It is an important thing to understand where you sit on the scale of your energy levels. To measure the intensity of your energy, the energy you are emitting, understand that every one of us has a unique signature generated purely by oneself. It is not too dissimilar to learning to write in primary school.

First, we learn to print, then we learn cursive or running writing. It's fascinating to watch how someone's written signature changes and evolves over time as you grow. Perhaps later in life one may marry as a woman and change her name completely and create a new signature entirely. Each progression is unique in its signature, defined solely by the relationship and understanding we have with our own energy at the time. Like a stamp, it indicates to others our strength, virility, voracity, intensity and often our intentions. Just like updating a wardrobe, it is a choice to create and continue to refine your style and expression of energy as your own unique signature.

This process is sadly not always a conscious one as it occurs with every thought and every feeling. Effects are not just limited to the mental and emotional realms either, as physical effects impact your field with every physical experience you have. The physical reality is intrinsically linked to the other subtle realms. From nourishing, healthy, vibrant food when compared with foods that are toxic or degrading your physicality, both have an effect on your energetics.

Similarly, you will be impacted by the places and spaces that you dwell and move amongst, as indeed your field is affected by the people you connect and associate with. Your energetic signature is unfolding and best described as an ever-dynamic imprint to the world. Just as one would sign one's name on a legal contract, the choices we make, the decisions we decide, and the intentions we set for ourselves will create, define and refine the impact of our signatures.

Once you are confident of your unique footprint, you will see how you influence other people's energies. Leaving imprints against their signature marks: affecting, creating, relating, changing, influencing surrounding energetics.

It is your soul's responsibility to understand how your energetic signature develops throughout your entire lifetime. As you become more aware and you focus on how you are presenting to the external world, a whole new layer of self-discovery will unfold.

What's most important is to understand that you alone are

the master of your signature. That you have a choice how you embellish your imprint, who you affect and how much you affect them. Will you choose a smooth gliding signature, or is it jagged and short? Perhaps your style is simple yet elegant, or perhaps highly charged or bold? Whatever you do, embrace it, nourish it, for a signature neglected is unreadable, distorted in an inadvertent way.

Choose a flavour of your making. Is it inviting, decisive, repellent or intimidating? One thing is for sure, your energetic signature is completely your creation. While many of us want to believe the power is outside of ourselves, the truth is, this is the only thing we have control over—how we wish to present our energy to the world.

"Act on your inner guidance and give up your need for proof that your inner guidance is authentic. The more you ask for proof, the less likely you are to receive any."
CAROLINE MYSS

YOUR INNER GUIDANCE SYSTEM

In the age of Google, we now ask our phones for many forms of guidance. Tell me where to eat, play me a song to listen to and how do I find my way to the next location. As we become more and more comfortable with artificial intelligence guiding us, we go further and further away from our own innate intelligence. Now please don't misunderstand me. I am a huge advocate for enhancing output with technological advancements, just not at the cost of understanding one's own inner nature.

There are many ways to connect with your inner guidance system. Some will be more obvious to you than others. Some may feel more natural than others, and some will be more powerful than others. Just like everything else in this book, your pathway to guidance is as unique as you are and is ultimately defined, refined and enhanced by you.

The experience of understanding what/who it is that guides you through life is exactly that it is experienced. We cannot buy it off a shelf or pre-order it. It must be recognised and claimed for oneself as uniquely tailored to you. It may engage a variety of different senses as some people are visual, so they will see things. Some people are auditory, so they may hear things. Some people are kinaesthetic, so they may feel things, and sometimes you don't know how, but you just know.

Over many years, I listened to many explanations about intuition. I continued to struggle to reconcile the depth of my life experiences that I still couldn't explain.

During the years, I realised my guidance system was particularly loud when I was off an optimal path. Increasingly, I tested this with reckless actions, producing louder and louder sirens that I was on a collision course. Any sane person would have heeded their calling. Yet strangely, as human nature will do, I needed to create undeniable proof that it warned me, and that I was defiantly ignoring my guidance of the imminent truth.

So, what do you require to be clear enough to understand your inner instructions against the ever-competing mind that will rationalise, hypothesise, distract and convince you otherwise?

Many people feel their guidance system in their gut and know instinctively that something is amiss or out of order. I have often heard one colleague say the hairs stand up on the back of his neck when he knows to avoid a situation.

Some describe it as an inner knowing or a sixth sense of something that feels true without evidence of the same. I have been fortunate in life to have been blessed with a colourful inner guidance, a knowing beyond knowing, without rational thinking something was 100% correct and true for me. Practice and much life experience eventually lead to the wisdom to finally listen to it.

So how do you connect to your guidance system?

1) You need a clear mind.

This statement is paradoxical given it's perhaps when we are not thinking clearly that we need our guidance volume up as much as possible.

There is no necessity to meditate *every* day, however, I am sure it assists many people greatly. The truth is that it's difficult to connect to anything when we are not clear. Meditation is one tool to clear the mind, as is nature, music and mindfulness. More vital than starting something new is to remove those things that currently create obstruction. This can range from eating poor quality junk food, alcohol, cigarettes, drugs, and poor thinking.

2) Be clear about your feelings:

Being in touch with one's feelings sounds simple, yet many of us have learned to suppress our unexpressed emotions, forming a habit of emotional disconnection. Given that often the inner guidance is a feeling-based experience, it makes it a challenge to be discerning if your emotional awareness is dulled or not fully operational.

3) Ask for it.

If you want to connect to your guidance system, you must turn the power switch on. If you do not ask for guidance, generally you will not receive it. On occasion, the divine will override and gift packets of information to every one of us, much like a booster signal overriding the radio channel that our guidance system operates on. Once again, as with so many things, our intention is powerful, so ask and then be willing to receive.

At this point comes the twist. You must be willing to receive the information in any format. Do not hold preconceived ideas about how it will be delivered for as soon as you dictate terms, the message will be distorted and more difficult to interpret. Understand how the signal presents on Monday may not be the way it presents on Tuesday or Wednesday. Also understand how guidance demonstrates to you will be different to Peter, Paul and Mary. The stories others share is exactly that—their stories.

It was once explained to me the general consensus is that this guidance is beyond what we know. It is not interpreted using the rational mind and therefore cannot be understood with the rational mind.

While the truth of our inner guidance system is that it comes from somewhere deep within, perhaps even beyond oneself, how you connect is a method for connecting to your own energy source.

When we are plugged into this connection and expression, we experience alignment and an innate sense of what is true, what isn't true and what's best to do, or what's better to avoid.

As you open to a new form of receiving guidance, experience will reinforce this channel of communication with your inner divine.

As you make choices with your inner guidance system, this will create evidence in the form of results that will then provide the format of the instructional manual, so to speak.

4) **Trust and keep trusting:**

If a car needs petrol to fuel the engine, then your guidance system needs trust. Interesting thing about trust is it's usually given in small doses to start. However, that's like starting the engine on little to no fuel. You won't get very far until the car stalls and you are left beside the road looking for help from others again. To kick start the journey, why not fill the tank right up? Invest in your success and have full faith in the process. You may correct your course a few times as you adjust to the steering, but soon you will be on the on-ramp to the freeway.

5) You must act upon your guidance.
As you define and strengthen your energetic signature, you will naturally develop its connection to your inner guidance. Just like an indication system in a car, the two are intrinsically linked. You cannot get on the on-ramp without making a turn onto it. As your guidance system sends you signals, your energetic signature will vary as you come across obstacles in your sphere of experience that are interacting with your energetic footprint.

Learning to view life from a perspective that is not fixed by logic is perhaps the most challenging part of the process. Connecting with one's own sense of how I know, when did I know, why is it that I know and what must I do now that I know. The Law of Divine Oneness states everything is connected. When your guidance system is turned on, you can gain insight and information from this field.

All guidance is inevitably a call to action, even if that be a restraint of action. Either way, a choice must be made, and a decision followed upon with no proof and no explanation.

In my early 20s, I was walking home from work one day through the busy streets of New York City. Out of nowhere, I heard a voice saying, "Do not walk your normal way home, walk across town." The feeling was so pure I didn't question it and altered my course immediately from my usual route home. A little later than usual, I arrived at my apartment building on the edge of the east village. It became clear from the commotion in the building that the gentleman in the foyer was in some distress kind.

Being New York, I heard him shriek, "It doesn't matter. I could have been killed," and swiftly closed his apartment door. The next morning, they placed a notice on the wall by the elevator warning all residents to be cautious to close the gate as there had been a mugging in the foyer. Instantly I had the realisation if I had not listened to that voice, I would have returned earlier and it would've been me who would have been mugged instead. Divine intervention or divine guidance. Either way, I am eternally grateful.

Sometimes it is easier to rationalise this as heavenly angels, beings or spirit guides who whisper in our ear, but the inner guidance knows when something is true.

The mind will bring many ideas and thoughts to us every day with which we have the choice to engage.

The inner guidance system is different to ideas and thoughts of the rational mind. I can't tell you how this will be true for you, but I can tell you that you will know when it is.

The mind intends to confuse and distract the soul, so ultimately, we all have to develop skills to tame the beast. A strong, clear connection to your own sense of inner guidance will hold you in good stead.

Start with something small, ask yourself, and be ready to receive it. When it feels true for you, take action and then review the results. You will soon know if you made your choice from your guidance system or from your mind. You cannot be in a place of fear and access your system. It's like a failsafe switch; it simply does not turn on.

So, when you operate in guidance, you will always experience amazing results.

You experience disappointment when you do not listen to

your inner guidance system, when you knew a person did not have the right intentions. Yet you allowed yourself to be influenced by them anyway for a seemingly logical decision.

Your guidance system may present new challenges and areas of growth; however, it will always ultimately take you into alignment. Just like Janet in The Good Place, think of it as an unlimited source of inner knowledge. Have some fun with it, give your system a name and personality. Ask yourself is it a female voice or a male voice that is speaking with you. Would you prefer to see it in maps and pictures or would you prefer to read it in braille, experiencing it with closed eyes and imagination only?

It is that part of yourself that you can call upon and command to show you what is the right thing for your soul.

Your inner guidance system is a dynamic system tailored solely to your unique life purpose. As do you work that nourishes it, the connection will grow stronger and clearer.

It will adapt depending on what it is you are asking it to guide you towards, however, this does not negate that you alone are accountable to walk your best path forward. When you take responsibility for the reality you create, you have just accessed the booster switch.

Sounds too good to be true? Well, trust me, there is not a soul on the planet who does not have their very own inner guidance system..

JOANNA JAMES

"Follow your bliss and the universe will open doors where there were only walls."
JOSEPH CAMPBELL

ACHIEVING YOUR BLISS

The most important word in the title is in the middle. "Your" bliss.

What is blissful to one person will be different for another.

The more we seek and search for bliss relative to how we think it should be, the more we rummage through the rubble of our broken dreams.

Bliss is beyond happiness, bliss is beyond joy, bliss is an experience of complete wonder, tailored uniquely to each soul. Bliss is when the soul is in alignment with the universe. There is no higher vibrational experience. It is the nirvana itself.

So many people on the planet look for things outside of themselves to elevate their mood, whether it be substances, emotions or sex. As experiences, they always fall short. Bliss is an energy generated from within and cannot be synthetically replicated, leaves no withdrawal, no dirty come down, only pure gratitude for the experience itself.

Bliss may arrive while sitting on the bank of the river or kiss your feet while doing the washing up. Moments of bliss come and go, irrespective of our external environment. Our natural way of being when we are young and pure of spirit is blissful, before we have concerns for the ways of the earthly world, dense in matter.

Life itself is a blissful thing. It's only when we become disconnected from life that we remove ourselves from this sense that is innate and natural to our being.

We then spend the rest of our time on planet Earth attempting to return, deciding the things we need to do to recreate it. When we realise that is flawed, we make decisions about the person we wish to be. Until, finally, we create the experiences that demonstrate we are moving into next level alignment.

When we are fully congruent with our true self, with whom we truly are in the moment and what life truly is in that split-second, we experience bliss.

This is when we can connect with the universal energetic field and experience the expansive energy of bliss.

It may be for a nanosecond, for minutes, or for hours, or even days.

One thing is for sure, we all seek bliss whether we are honest about it as it is our natural state of being.

So, we can leave it to chance, or we can get to work on elevating our vibration in preparation.

Start with those things that lower your vibration such as:
- negative thoughts
- destructive emotions
- substances that suppress
- Spaces and places that have any fields of energetic disturbances

Even after you do all the above, seeking bliss holds no guarantees. It will require unwavering belief, thoughts repeatedly charged with emotions - otherwise known as faith. Because it requires faith to have your heart and mind in total alignment.

To copy or replicate the experience is futile, for bliss cannot be recreated. It is unique. Rather than expectation, it requires surrender to be fully present. This is why gratitude is such a handy springboard, for when we are in gratitude, we cannot be in fear.

To be fully present with the energy of bliss, it requires going beyond love; it requires shifting beyond matter into vibrational form itself. Perhaps this is why the feeling is so incredible. The physical tingling is the recognition of intense vibrating energy.

So once you have experienced bliss, what do you do?.

"When the basis for your actions is inner alignment with the present moment, your actions become empowered by the intelligence of life itself."

ECKHART TOLLE

NEXT LEVEL ALIGNMENT

When you review the Law of Cause and Effect, the enormous responsibility dawns upon us that we each have an effect with everything we think, everything we say, and everything we do.

Just like ripples across a lakeside, we are balls of energy transmitting signal 24/7. The effect we have is well beyond what we can measure day to day.

Marianne Williamson encapsulated this perfectly when she said:

"Our deepest fear is not that we are inadequate. Our deepest fear is that we are powerful beyond measure."

Our impact reverberates externally, whether we are conscious of how we deliver our impact or not.

So how do I get to the Next Level of Alignment in Life?

Whether it be a better, more loving relationship, a better, more successful career, more financial abundance, or a deeper spiritual understanding, perhaps the more poignant question is what happens when we don't? What is the true effect of not living a life in alignment and how could that be measured? If it comprises the vast unknown of what might have been one, or a series of possible realities? Another way of explaining this is your Next Level Alignment is whatever you choose it to be, so consider your choices wisely.

Along the roadside to alignment we make many pits stops where we evaluate our progress by identifying our location on a scale of extremes, rich-poor, weak-strong, good-bad. We live in a world of polarity. This Universal Law states that everything has an equal opposite. At any moment we can slide along the scale and choose if we will vibrate in harmony with one end or the other.

The more we focus on where we are, the more we create more of where we are. The more we focus on where we want to be, the faster we will move there.

Sounds simple, right?

In the very moment our thoughts and feelings are congruent, as if the potential reality is real, it will be. Living a life of Next Level Alignment is a step-by-step practice in creating the reality you choose moment to moment 24/7. Sound familiar?

Mastering this process takes dedication and focus, when we are easily distracted with the day to day. Which is why a comprehensive study of the Mind, the Body and Spaces helps us gain clarity on what we are truly choosing to create.

As I sit here finalising this book, the world is deep in the outbreak of the Corona Virus. Australia is submerging into fear as borders close, and isolations start. There is no more challenging time to write about creating a life of Next level Alignment, when facing fear on a mass scale. Napoleon Hill said, "That every adversity has the seed of equal or greater opportunity." This is a direct understanding of polarity and possibility. Perhaps the next time we are faced with world challenges, we may take a moment to consider the potential of the equally opposite reality. If everything is energy, then we can choose at any time the frequency with which we are vibrating, regardless of the immediate surroundings. This to me is self-mastery.

So, what frequency shall we choose?
A choice implies a process by which we must compare or evaluate to make a decision. The Universal Law of Relativity states that nothing is good or bad until we view it in comparison. This leads us back to the introduction of this book and the exploration that life is a giant spiral. Life is energy, it has no quality on its own, it just is what it is.

However, this energy is expressed, it is all the same origin. The way in which we judge our progress or make meaning in life is typically by placing things into comparison to other things. When you consider that everything is connected, you can see that we are all a part of the same. We are one.

We, you, I each participate in life to add, change, or vary the energy of everything around us. It is from this fundamental understanding that we can be empowered to create a life of Next *Level of Alignment*, not just individually, but in connection with all that is.

Remember, Alignment is what *you* determine Alignment to be, governed according to Universal Laws, and demonstrated through the interplay of Mind, Body and Spaces..

THE 12 UNIVERSAL LAWS IN SIMPLE EXPLANATION.

1. Law of Divine Oneness - absolutely everything is connected.
2. Law of Vibration - everything is in motion and has a unique energy signature.
3. Law of Correspondence - all patterns repeat form - so above is below.
4. Law of Attraction – like attracts like.
5. Law of Inspired Action - we must actively pursue goals.
6. Law of perpetual Transmutation of Energy - everything is in a state of constant change.
7. Law of Cause and Effect - all action has a corresponding reaction.
8. Law of Compensation - you receive what you give.
9. Law of Relativity- nothing is good or bad until viewed in comparison.
10. Law of Polarity - everything has an equal opposite.
11. Law of Rhythm - everything moves in cycles.
12. Law of Gender - there is always a Yin and Yang..

REFERENCES :

MOULD and Water Damaged Buildings:

- Fisk WJ, Lei-Gomez Q, Mendell MJ, "Association of residential dampness and mould with respiratory tract infections and bronchitis: a meta-analysis." Environmental Health Review 2010, www.ehjournal.net/content9/1/72
- Fisk WJ, Lei Gomez Q, Mendell MJ, "Meta-analyses of the associations of respiratory health effects with dampness and mould in homes", Indoor Air. 2007 Aug;17(4):284-96.
- Flannigan B, Samson RA, Miller JD (2011). Microorganisms in home and indoor work environments: diversity, health impacts, investigation and control. CRC Press. Boca Raton, FL. pp. 147-182.
- https://www.medicalnewstoday.com/articles/320331.php#1 Antova T[1], Pattenden S, Brunekreef B, Heinrich J, Rudnai P, Forastiere F, Luttmann-Gibson H, Grize L, Katsnelson B, Moshammer H, Nikiforov B, Slachtova H, Slotova K, Zlotkowska R, Fletcher T, 2008 Aug;62(8):708-14. doi: 10.1136/jech.2007.065896,
- *Exposure to indoor mould and children's respiratory health in the PATY study*, Environmental Health Unit, NCPHP, Sofia, Bulgaria
- *Aspergillus species in indoor environments and their possible occupational and public health hazards* B Mousavi,[1,2] MT Hedayati,[*,1,2] N Hedayati,[3] M Ilkit,[4] and S Syedmousavi[5,6,7,1]
- *The Myth of Mycotoxins and Mould Injury.*
Chang C[1,2], Gershwin ME[3].
https://www.ncbi.nlm.nih.gov/pubmed/31608429

- Australian College of Environmental Studies manual v6 2018
- https://www.ncbi.nlm.nih.gov/pmc/articles/PMC5490296/
- https://www.ncbi.nlm.nih.gov/pubmed/?term=antova+t+-exposure+to+mold

EMF:

- http://www.powerwatch.org.uk/
- http://www.bioinitiative.org/table-of-contents/
- http://reset.me/story/the-alarming-ways-emfs-are-changing-your-brain/
- https://www.ncbi.nlm.nih.gov/pubmed/15182885
- http://international-emf-alliance.org/
- http://www.radiationresearch.org/pdfs/rncnirp_children.pdf

Hypersensitivity

- https://en.wikipedia.org/wiki/Electromagnetic_hypersensitivity
- Bevington, M. (2013). Electromagnetic sensitivity and Electromagnetic Hypersensitivity. A Summary. Capability Books.
- ECERI. (2015). Idiopathic environmental intolerance. Paris Appeal. 18 May 2015. Royal Academy of Medicine, Belgium. Read pages 14 to 23 and 32 to 40

- EUROPAEM EMF Guideline 2015 for the prevention, diagnosis and treatment of EMF-related health problems and illnesses.
- De Luca et al. (2014). Metabolic and genetic screening of EHS subjects. Mediators Inflam

Printed in Australia
AUHW020749280621
347765AU00001B/1

9 780648 883982